The Easter Tree

Discover the pictures of Easter as you read the story of Jesus

Veronica Heley

Published by
The Bible Reading Fellowship
Peter's Way, Sandy Lane West
Oxford OX4 5HG
ISBN 1 84101 085 5
First published 2000
10 9 8 7 6 5 4 3 2 1

Acknowledgments
Unless otherwise stated, scripture quotations are taken from the Good News Bible published by The Bible Societies/HarperCollins Publishers Ltd, UK © American Bible Society 1966, 1971, 1976, 1992, used with permission.

A catalogue record for this book is available from the British Library

Printed and bound in Malta by Interprint Limited

Introduction

The Easter Tree has pictures of Jesus' Easter story.

In the days before Easter, as you read the story of what happened to Jesus, imagine yourself there. Look for the picture of a child wearing trainers… there's one in every story!

Find the symbol for that day's story in the picture. Turn to the centre of the book, find the symbol for that day on the Easter tree, and colour it in.

1

Mary took half a litre of a very expensive perfume made of pure nard, poured it on Jesus' feet, and wiped them with her hair.
John 12:3

What a waste!

Imagine you are there when Jesus and his friends go to a party. Perhaps you are helping to look after the guests. Suddenly, Jesus' friend Mary comes in and pours a precious perfume made from a plant called spikenard—nard for short—over Jesus' feet. The perfume fills the house. Can you see how she dries his feet?

Judas is always thinking of ways to make money. He grumbles, 'What a waste!'

Jesus says, 'Leave her alone. She did this because she loves me.'

So it wasn't such a waste after all, was it?

Prayer

Dear Jesus, show me what I can do to please you today. Amen

A large crowd of people spread their cloaks on the road, while others cut branches from the trees and spread them on the road.
Matthew 21:8

2 A day to remember

Most of us have someone we like to be with on special days—like birthdays.

Jesus and his friends were going to Jerusalem for a special holy day. Jesus said, 'In the next village you'll find a donkey tied up with her colt beside her. Bring them here. If anyone asks what you're doing, say, "The master needs them", and he will let them go.'

Jesus' friends found the animals just as he'd said. They threw their cloaks over the donkey and Jesus got on. People crowded around to cheer him on his way. Can you see what they are spreading in his path?

The crowds shouted, 'Praise the Lord!'

Prayer

Dear Jesus, help me to praise you today and every day. Amen

Jesus said, 'You see this grain of wheat? Here in my hand it is no more than a single grain. But if it is sown in the soil it becomes a plant which bears many other grains.'

John 12:24 (adapted)

A new life

Here is Jesus walking in the countryside with some of his friends. He is telling them what is going to happen to him. He holds up an ear of wheat, and reminds them that being planted in the ground is the only way it will grow into many more plants.

The meaning behind this story is that although Jesus was to die here on earth, his death would not be the end but the start of new life with him for us—a new life which starts here and now.

3

5

Prayer

Dear Jesus, help me to understand that your death was a beginning, not an end. Amen

'As you go into the city, a man carrying a jar of water will meet you. Follow him into the house that he enters, and say to the owner of the house, "The Teacher says to you, Where is the room where my disciples and I will eat the Passover meal?"'

Luke 22:10–11

Following instructions

Peter and John need to know where Jesus plans to eat their special holiday meal. Jesus says, 'As you enter Jerusalem, you'll see a man carrying a water jar…'

Peter and John are puzzled. Men didn't fetch water! That was women's work!

But, following Jesus' instructions, they go to the city gate, which is guarded by Roman soldiers. And can you see what they see next?

They go with the man into a big house, and up the stairs into a large room. There they get ready for the meal.

4

Prayer

Dear Jesus, help me to follow your instructions. Amen

Jesus said, 'You are like light for the whole world. A city built on a hill cannot be hidden.'

Matthew 5:14

5 Showing love for others

Imagine turning on a light at home, and then covering it over with a box. What use would the light be then? We put it where it lights up the whole room, don't we?

In the same way, our inner light must shine out so that everyone can see the good that we do because we love Jesus.

Jesus said that we must shine with a pure, clear light, and not try to hide it. In the same way, the city of Jerusalem was built on a hill so that everyone could see it for miles around.

See how the girl in the picture is like a light in the darkness, because she's helping others.

Prayer

Dear Jesus, help me to show everyone how much I love you. Amen

When they arrived in Jerusalem, Jesus went to the temple and began to drive out all those who were buying and selling. He overturned the tables of the money-changers and the stools of those who sold pigeons.
Mark 11:15

In God's house

Jesus is angry. The temple is God's house for prayer and praise. But here are people selling animals, and the pigeons which are used to pay for temple services. There are even some bankers, changing money for foreign tourists! Many are cheating their customers.

Jesus drives them all out of the temple, saying, 'God's temple is meant to be a house of prayer, but you have turned it into a den of thieves!'

See how the children laugh with delight to see the pigeons flying free in God's house.

Prayer

Dear Jesus, help me to respect the places set aside for prayer and praise to God. Amen

6

One of the twelve disciples—the one named Judas Iscariot—went to the chief priests and asked, 'What will you give me if I betray Jesus to you?' They counted out thirty silver coins and gave them to him.

Matthew 26:14–15

Never let a friend down

7

It is very upsetting to be let down by a friend. Perhaps it has happened to you.

Judas is one of Jesus' friends. His job is to look after the money for everyone. Judas will do anything for money.

Judas knows the chief priests want to get rid of Jesus. But they can't manage it because Jesus is so popular. Judas secretly visits the chief priests and arranges for Jesus to be arrested.

The chief priests are delighted. They promise to pay Judas a large sum of money. Now Judas has to find a way to hand Jesus over without the people knowing.

Can you see which boy is cheating?

Prayer

Dear Jesus, help me never to let a friend down. Amen

Jesus poured some water into a basin and began to wash the disciples' feet and dry them with the towel round his waist.
John 13:5

8

Look after one another

It is evening in the Upper Room. The lamps have been lit, and all Jesus' friends are here for the special holiday meal. We know Jesus is a very special person, so we peep round the door to see what is happening.

No one sits down to supper without first washing their feet, because the street outside is so dusty. Usually a servant sees to this, but now Jesus himself is doing it, not just for himself but for all his friends, too!

No wonder Peter protests. 'That's a job for servants!'

Jesus smiles. 'Look after one another, serve one another, just as I have been looking after you,' he says.

Prayer

Dear Lord Jesus, help us to look after one another. Amen

Soon I will leave you. You will look for me, but you cannot go where I am going. Now I want to give you a new commandment; love one another. That way, everyone will know that you are friends of mine.

John 13:33–35 (adapted)

Following Jesus

Everyone is having a good time until Jesus starts talking about leaving us. None of us wants that to happen.

Peter says it for all of us. 'Why can't I follow you? I'm ready to die for you!'

Sadly Jesus says, 'Are you really ready to die for me? Before the cock crows at dawn, you will say three times that you don't know me.'

Prayer

Dear Jesus, help me to follow your example and love other people, even though that can be very hard to do. I know that you will always hold my hand to help me to follow you. Amen

9

10

Jesus took a cup, gave thanks to God, and said, 'Take this and share it among yourselves...' Then he took a piece of bread, gave thanks to God, broke it and gave it to them, saying, 'This is my body which is given for you. Do this in memory of me.'

Luke 22:17 and 19

Do this in memory of me

The lamps are burning low. The party is nearly over. Jesus watches as his old friend Judas slides out of the room. Jesus knows what Judas is going to do. It is nearly time to go.

This is the last time Jesus is to eat with his friends. Do you see the bread and wine on the table in front of Jesus? He lifts his hands and prays over them, giving us one more way to remember him.

Prayer

Dear Lord Jesus, help me to remember everything you've taught us. Amen

Jesus prayed, 'My Father! All things are possible for you. Take this cup of suffering away from me. Yet not what I want, but what you want.'
Mark 14:36

The hardest prayer

The moon is bright as we leave the Upper Room to walk in one of Jesus' favourite places, where olive trees grow on the hillside just outside Jerusalem.

Jesus asks his best friends—Peter, James and John—to keep watch while he prays. But after such a good party, they curl up under the trees and go to sleep.

Jesus knows what's going to happen. It's almost too much for him to bear. See how hard he prays!

Tonight of all nights he needs his friends but they can't stay awake long enough to help him. Three times he finds them asleep… and then it is too late…

11

Prayer

Dear God, help me to know when my friends need me to pray for them. Amen

Judas had given the crowd a signal:
'The man I kiss is the one you want.
Arrest him and take him away under guard.'
Mark 14:44

Arrested!

All is quiet under the trees in the moonlight. Suddenly Judas arrives with a group of men carrying torches. They have come from the chief priests to arrest Jesus, and are armed with swords and clubs. Judas kisses Jesus.

The guards look anxious as they close in on Jesus. But there is no need, for you can see that all his friends are running away in fright or hiding behind the trees. Only Peter draws a sword and strikes out at the high priest's slave, cutting off his ear. But then even Peter runs away.

Jesus touches the man's ear and heals it.

12

Prayer

Loving Lord, help me to be kind even to those who want to hurt me. Amen

The Roman soldiers with their commanding officer and the Jewish guards arrested Jesus, bound him, and took him for trial.
John 18:12–13

13

Taken away!

The moonlit garden is no longer peaceful. Jesus' friends have run away and he is surrounded by armed guards, who hold him tightly between them. The guards are still afraid, even though Jesus is not armed. One of his friends had drawn a sword, but that small show of defiance was soon over.

Can you see who is hiding behind the trees? Some of Jesus' friends are too afraid to go to his rescue, but they can't bear to leave him altogether. Now they have to watch as the guards use cruelly hard ropes to bind Jesus before they hustle him away.

Peter and one other of Jesus' friends follow… at a distance.

Prayer

Dear Jesus, help me to stand by my friends if they get into trouble. Amen

The Easter Tree

Find the symbol for today and colour it in.

INRI

'Before the cock crows tonight you, Peter, will say three times that you do not know me.'
Luke 22:61

14

Peter's denial

The high priest's house is lit by many lamps as Jesus is put on trial, and in the courtyard the servants huddle around a big fire.

Peter can't get into the house to hear what is happening, so he joins the group round the fire. One of the women recognizes Peter as a friend of Jesus. Afraid, Peter says he doesn't know Jesus.

Later a man accuses Peter of knowing Jesus, and finally another servant points the finger at Peter. Peter still denies it… but at that very moment a cock crows. Dawn is breaking over the city.

Inside the house, Jesus turns and looks through the doorway at Peter. Peter realizes what he's done. He's horrified and rushes outside in distress.

Prayer

Dear Lord, help me never to say I don't know you—when in my heart I do. Amen

When Pilate saw that... a riot might break out, he took some water, washed his hands in front of the crowd, and said, 'I am not responsible for the death of this man!'

Matthew 27:24

Pilate washes his hands

Early in the morning the chief priests take Jesus in chains to the Roman governor, Pontius Pilate. They tell Pilate that Jesus is breaking Roman law, claiming to be king of the Jews.

Pilate is not fooled and plans to release Jesus, but the chief priests arrange that the mob should shout for Jesus to be put to death. Pilate says that he can release Jesus or a murderer called Barabbas. The crowd shout for Barabbas to be released, and for Jesus to die.

Prayer

Dear God, I know that washing my hands of a problem doesn't make it go away. Help me to stand up for those in the right, even when everyone else is against them. Amen

15

Then Pilate set Barabbas free for them; and after he had Jesus whipped, he handed him over to be crucified.
Matthew 27:26

16 The crowd have their way

Pilate only gave in to the high priests because he thought the crowd would get out of hand and riot. But he is not happy about it.

Barabbas is happy. He laughs out loud as he runs out of the palace and is lost in the crowd. Barabbas is a murderer and deserves to die, while Jesus is taken into the governor's palace to be punished when he has done nothing wrong. Can you see what the guard with Jesus is holding?

The chief priests are happy, too. They have arranged for Jesus to die as if he were a common criminal, and that will be the end of him. Or so they think!

Prayer

Dear Jesus, help me never to let anyone else be punished for my wrongdoing. Amen

They made a crown out of thorny branches and placed it on his head, and put a stick in his right hand; then they knelt before him and mocked him.
Matthew 27:29

The crown of thorns

No one likes to be made fun of, do they?

Inside the governor's palace the soldiers take off Jesus' own robe and dress him in a scarlet one. One soldier makes a crown out of thorny twigs, and places it on Jesus' head. Another puts a stick instead of a royal sceptre in Jesus' hand. Then they play a game with him. Kneeling down, they mock him, saying, 'Long live the King of the Jews!'

When the soldiers get tired of playing this game, they take off the scarlet robe and give Jesus back his own clothes.

17

Prayer

Loving Lord, help me never to hurt anyone by making fun of them or by calling them rude names. Amen

They met a man from Cyrene named Simon, and
the soldiers forced him to carry Jesus' cross.
Matthew 27:32

Simon of Cyrene

Next morning the soldiers lead Jesus out of the city and give him part of his cross to carry. It is very heavy. Lots of people come out of Jerusalem to watch.

Everyone can see that Jesus is not able to carry the heavy piece of wood all the way. What are the soldiers going to do about it? They look for someone in the crowd who can help Jesus. They pick on a big, strong man called Simon, who has just come in from the country to sell his goods. Simon dare not refuse the soldiers, but through carrying Jesus' cross he comes to know and love him.

Prayer

Thank you Jesus that, like Simon, I can find you in the most unexpected of places. Amen

18

19

They came to a place called Golgotha, which means, 'The Place of the Skull'. There they offered Jesus wine mixed with a bitter substance; but after tasting it, he would not drink it. They crucified him...
Matthew 27:33–35

The Place of the Skull

At last they arrive at the bare hillside where criminals are brought to die. It has an ugly name—The Place of the Skull.

On top of the hill, some tall posts have been driven deep into the ground. The soldiers take Jesus to the centre post. They can see how tired he is. They are sorry for him, and offer him a drink before they nail him to the crossbar and haul it to the top of the post.

Can you see some friends of Jesus trudging up the hill to be near him at this terrible time?

Prayer

Dear Lord, never let me forget what you went through for me. Amen

They took the robe, which was made of one piece of woven cloth without any seams in it. The soldiers said to one another, 'Let's not tear it; let's throw dice to see who will get it.'
John 19:23–24

Throwing dice

The sun climbs high as Jesus hangs on the cross. To pass the time, the soldiers sit down to divide his clothes between them. Jesus has one very good piece of clothing, so they throw dice to see who should keep it.

Some of the oldest games in the world use dice, which were usually made of bone. The Roman soldiers often play with them.

24

Jesus' mother Mary and two of her friends have come to be near him. Jesus' friend John is also there. Jesus asks John to look after his mother for him.

20

Prayer

Dear Lord, show me how to look after those you love. Amen

Pilate wrote a notice and had it put on the cross. 'Jesus of Nazareth, the King of the Jews.'
John 19:19

King of the Jews

21

Long ago, children who didn't behave in class were given a paper hat to wear with a large D on it, for 'Dunce'. Everyone laughed at the dunce.

In the same way, the Romans wrote a man's crime on a board and hung it on the cross. Can you see the notice on Jesus' cross? Pilate doesn't believe Jesus has done anything wrong, so he has written 'The King of the Jews' in Hebrew, Latin and Greek, or INRI for short.

The chief priests want Pilate to change it, but he refuses. So everyone who passes by can read that Jesus is the King of the Jews. Some jeer, but others are sad.

Prayer

Dear God, help me never to laugh at anyone unkindly. Amen

They crucified Jesus there, and the two criminals, one on his right and the other on his left.
Luke 23:33

The two thieves

It's never too late to say you're sorry.

High on the hillside stand three crosses. On either side of Jesus hang two thieves. One shouts and swears at Jesus, saying, 'If you really are the King of the Jews, then save yourself and us!'

But the other one says, 'How dare you speak to him like that! We're only getting what we deserve, but he hasn't done anything wrong!'

This second thief says to Jesus, 'Remember me, when you come again as King.'

Jesus can see that the man is sorry for what he has done. He says, 'Today you will be in heaven with me.'

22

Prayer

Dear Father God, help me to say I'm sorry when I've done something wrong. Amen

23

Jesus drank the wine and said, 'It is finished!'
Then he bowed his head and died.
John 19:30

Jesus dies

It is very hot. The sun beats down on the bare hillside where Jesus hangs on the cross. He is near to death.

Jesus murmurs, 'I am thirsty.' One of the soldiers soaks a sponge in the bowl of cheap wine they are sharing. He puts the sponge on a long stalk taken from a bush nearby, and holds it up so that Jesus can taste the wine.

Jesus tastes the wine, bows his head and says, 'It is finished.' It is not the wine that is finished. It is Jesus' job of preparing the way for us to be friends with God, now and for ever.
This is why Jesus died.

Prayer

Dear Jesus, thank you that you died for me. Amen

24 Darkness!

It was about twelve o'clock when the sun stopped shining and darkness covered the whole country until three o'clock.
Luke 23:44

Did you hear about the sun's eclipse? Perhaps you actually saw it happen?

When Jesus dies the moon moves across the sun, the birds stop singing, and the air grows cold. The last rays of the sun fall across Jesus' face, and light up those of his mother Mary and his friend, John, standing nearby.

The soldiers don't understand what is happening. Can you see what one of them has done in his fright? All those who had come out to watch Jesus die hurry home, sad and afraid.

But this is no ordinary eclipse. The sun doesn't shine out again for three hours. Afterwards, a man called Joseph of Arimathea goes to Pilate and asks permission to bury Jesus' body.

Prayer

Dear Lord, help me never to be afraid of the dark. Amen

There was a garden in the place where Jesus had been put to death, and in it there was a new tomb where no one had ever been buried... Because the tomb was close by, they placed Jesus' body there.

John 19:41–42

The tomb

Jesus loved gardens. At dusk Joseph and a friend place Jesus' body in a tomb in a nearby garden. As they leave, the soldiers lever a huge rock over the doorway, so that nobody can get in.

Meanwhile, the gardener goes home after a hard day's work.

Can you see something which looks like an egg in the picture? Eggs used to be a big treat and were saved up to eat at Easter. That is why it is extra special to have an egg which is made of chocolate at Easter.

25

Prayer

Dear Jesus, help me to remember you when I eat an egg at Easter. Amen

Early on Sunday morning, while it was still dark, Mary Magdalene went to the tomb and saw that the stone had been taken away from the entrance.

John 20:1

Empty!

Jesus died on a Friday, and Saturday was a day of rest when no work could be done. So it is early on Sunday morning when Mary Magdalene visits the tomb. Birds are singing, flowers are opening... but what is this?

The stone has gone from the tomb, and so have the soldiers! See where they dropped their weapons as they fled.

Jesus told his friends many times that he would die and rise again from the dead. But they didn't understand. They saw him die and thought, 'Well, that's the end of that!'

Mary runs to tell his friends that someone has stolen Jesus!

Prayer

Dear Jesus, help me to remember and understand when I learn something important about you.

26

27

Simon Peter saw the linen wrappings lying there and the cloth which had been round Jesus' head. It was not lying with the linen wrappings but was rolled up by itself.
John 20:6–7

The gardener

The sun is up by the time Simon Peter and John come running to the tomb. Mary hurries along behind. They look into the tomb. Everything is exactly as Mary has told them. They can't understand it! The tomb is empty, except for the linen that had been wrapped around Jesus' body.

As the two men return home, worried and upset, Mary sees someone whom she thinks is the gardener. She begs him to tell her what he's done with Jesus' body. But it is Jesus himself. He says, 'Mary!' and she knows him at once. He says, 'Go and tell the others…'

Prayer

Loving Lord, help me to remember all the marvellous things you did. Amen

It was late that Sunday evening, and the disciples were gathered together behind locked doors, because they were afraid of the Jewish authorities. Then Jesus came and stood among them. 'Peace be with you,' he said.
John 20:19

The very best party

Jesus' friends are afraid that the soldiers might want to arrest them, too. So that evening when they meet together in the room where they had last seen Jesus, they lock the heavy door, and take out the key.

Some say that Jesus has been seen alive. What can it all mean?

And then, even though the door is locked, Jesus himself is standing among them! Once they get over their shock and make sure it really is him, they push back the table and dance and sing! Everything Jesus promised has come true! What a party this is!

28

Prayer

Jesus is risen, Alleluia.